SYSTEMS OF GOVERNMENT

COMMUNISM

R. G. Grant

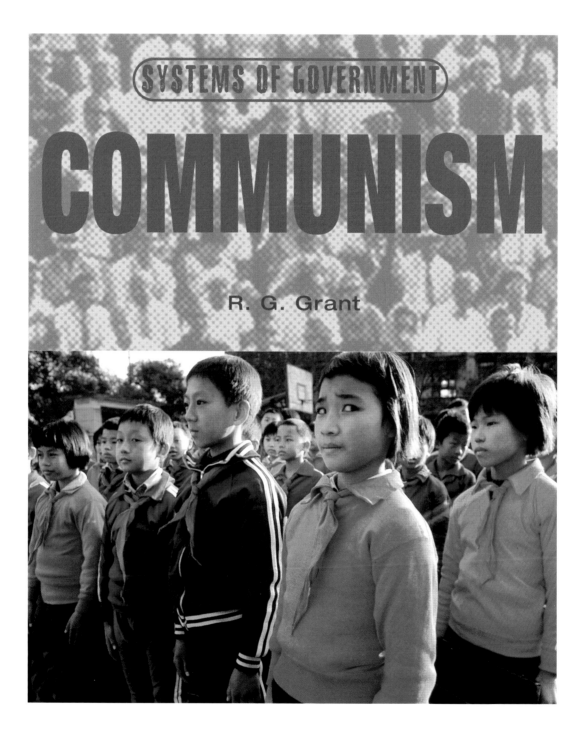

Evans

Published by Evans Brothers Limited
2A Portman Mansions
Chiltern Street
London W1U 6NR

Planned and produced for Evans Brothers by Book Factory Limited.

First published 2005

British Library Cataloguing in Publication Data
Grant, R.G
Communism. - (Systems of government)
1. Communism - Juvenile literature
2. Communism - History - Juvenile literature
I. Title
320.5'32

Published and bound by A.G.G. Printing Stars

ISBN 0237526999

Editor: Patience Coster
Designer: Jane Hawkins
Illustrations: Stefan Chabluk
Consultant: Michael Rawcliffe

We are grateful to the following for permission to reproduce photographs: Antoine Gyori/Corbis Sygma 43; Bettman/Corbis 16, 23; Corbis 7, 14; Dave Bartruff/Corbis 25 (*above*); Elio Ciol/Corbis *front cover* and 4; Françoise de Mulder/Corbis 19; Guang Niu/Reuters/Corbis 20; Jacques Langevin/Corbis Sygma 24, 39; Keran Su/Corbis 42; Keystone/Getty Images 13; Les Stone/Corbis 32; Noboru Hashimoto/Corbis/Sygma 8; Owen Franken/Corbis *title page* and 29; Peter Turnley/Corbis 31; Topham/Associated Press 22, 25 (*below*), 28, 37; Topham/ImageWorks 5, 27, 41; Topham Picturepoint 10, 11, 12, 17, 33, 34, 35; Topham/Public Record Office/HIP 18; Wally McNamee/Corbis 38, 40; Yevgeny Khaldei/Corbis *front cover*.

CONTENTS

CHAPTER 1

What is Communism?

To understand the nature of the communist systems of government that exist in the world today, we first need to look at what communism was ideally meant to be. Communism was intended to be a system of government brought about by a workers' revolution that would take power away from the middle class (bourgeoisie). The result would be a government that ran factories and businesses for the benefit of the workers, ending the system of labour for private profit. In its ideal form, communism would lead eventually to a state of perfect equality, freedom and self-fulfilment for all people. The communist systems of government that exist in the world today are the remnants of an extraordinary project that aimed at nothing less than the transformation of human life.

"The workers have nothing to lose... but their chains. They have a world to gain. Workers of the world, unite!"

The final words of The Communist Manifesto, *published by Karl Marx and Friedrich Engels in 1848.*

The origins of communism

Modern communism has its origins in the revolutionary ideas of Karl Marx, a nineteenth-century thinker and writer. Marx lived at a time when, especially in Western Europe and North America, the Industrial Revolution was radically changing the

In Leningrad (now St Petersburg), Russia, in the days of the communist Soviet Union, a parade marches past a huge banner showing (left to right) Marx, Engels and Lenin.

way most people lived and worked. Instead of working on farms in the country, more and more people were living in towns and working in factories. The new factories were generating immense wealth for their owners who invested their money (capital) in machinery to make a profit. This system, in which wealthy people invested money in order to make more money, became known as 'capitalism'. The workers who laboured for the capitalist owners in the factories endured harsh working conditions and lived in relative poverty.

In the year 2000, Vietnam was still a communist state. Here schoolchildren visit the tomb of revered former Vietnamese communist leader Ho Chi Minh in Hanoi.

Combining ideas from other thinkers with his own original concepts, Marx developed a revolutionary view of history which he believed made sense of what was happening around him. He described history as the story of conflict between social classes – each class being a group of individuals with similar economic interests. In Marx's view there had always been one class that oppressed and exploited the rest of society. In nineteenth-century Western Europe and North America, power was in the hands of businessmen and factory owners – the 'bourgeoisie'. They built up their wealth by exploiting the industrial workers – the working class or 'proletariat'. The proletariat were people who had nothing to sell but their labour which, according to Marx, was bought by the factory owners for less than its real value.

Marx believed that the working class was destined one day to seize control of the state, ending the capitalist system of exploitation of the workers by the bourgeoisie. Once in power, the workers would take over the economy and unleash the full productive potential of industrialisation, eventually building a world in which there was such abundance of goods that everyone could have their needs fulfilled. This would be a 'communist' society, in which there would be no

KARL MARX

Born in Trier, Germany, in 1818, Karl Marx was a revolutionary thinker and a political activist. In 1848, with his colleague Friedrich Engels, he published *The Communist Manifesto*, calling for industrial workers to seize power in a revolution. The following year Marx moved to London, where he spent the rest of his life. He played a leading role in setting up the First International Working Men's Association in 1864. Intended to unite workers from different countries to fight against the existing order of society, the First International was in reality bitterly divided and fell apart in 1872. Marx was much more successful as a writer than in practical politics. The first volume of his major work, *Das Kapital (Capital)*, was published in 1867. A massive analysis of the capitalist economic system, it later became the bible of the communist movement. Marx died in 1883.

private property and in which life would be based on equality, justice and cooperation. What Marxists called 'the exploitation of man by man' would come to an end and humans would for the first time be able to fulfil their true creative potential.

Radical change

Marx's ideas became massively influential after his death, especially in mainland Europe (less so in Britain and in the United States). Shaped into a set of beliefs known as 'Marxism', they were an inspiration to would-be revolutionaries, who looked forward to a violent overthrow of existing society. They also appealed to many parliamentary socialists – people who also wanted a radical change in society but who hoped to gain power by winning a majority of votes in elections.

Marx's analysis of history and society was believed by his admirers to show scientifically that the capitalist system would eventually collapse. His vision of a future 'communist' world, however vague, was a positive goal towards which people could struggle. Marx had not, however, spent a lot of time working out how exactly a people's state would be run. His writings did not give a precise or detailed plan for a new system of government; but he was certain that after the workers' revolution the state would in time 'wither away'.

In the ideal communist world, there would be no more need of police or law courts or armies. Marx also assumed that, first, the revolutionary workers would have to dispossess the bourgeoisie – in other words, take from them their property. It was ownership of this property, Marx argued, that enabled the bourgeoisie to control and dominate society. Marx's plan suggested the need for a strong state system, at least temporarily, since the bourgeoisie was unlikely to accept being dispossessed without a struggle. On issues such as these, Marx's writings gave little solid guidance.

Marxist-Leninism

It was only when Marxist revolutionaries managed for the first time actually to seize and hold power – in the Russian Empire from 1917 – that what can be referred to as a communist system of government was invented. The leader of the Russian

---

Socialism and communism

The use of the terms 'socialism' and 'communism' can be confusing. Historically, the communist movement is part of the wider movement of socialism. This is made up of all those political groups who have wanted to improve the lot of working people, and curb the power of wealthy individuals, by putting at least part, if not all, of the economy under some form of state or communal ownership.

Since communist systems of government emerged, the term 'socialist' has often been used for 'democratic socialists' – those, such as the British Labour Party, prepared to work within the rules of liberal democracy. In this way, 'socialists' are distinguished from 'communists' with their tradition of single-party rule. In Marxist theory, however, 'socialism' is the term for a transitional stage between capitalism and communism. Since no state has so far claimed to implement communism fully, countries under communist rule habitually refer to their own stage of development as 'socialism'.

revolutionary regime was Vladimir Ilyich Lenin, and the theory and practice of government that developed in Russia after 1917 is often called Marxist-Leninism. With small variants this system, developed under the specific conditions of the Russian Revolution (*see Chapter 2*), was subsequently applied in many other countries during the twentieth century.

Its central feature was the rule of a single political party – the Communist Party – which held a monopoly of power in all areas of society. In theory, the ruling party represented, and acted on behalf of, the working masses – it was the 'vanguard of the proletariat'. Its mission was to transform society in line with Marxist ideas. Education, culture and the media were all placed under strict party control and used to provide propaganda for the revolutionary cause.

Communism in the Soviet Union

From 1923, the countries of the former Russian Empire became known as the Soviet Union. Communists in power in the Soviet Union and elsewhere achieved part of the Marxist dream (*see page 13*). Industry, banking, trade and land were taken out of the hands of private individuals or companies and put under state ownership. Instead of a free market economy, in which goods are produced for profit and sold for whatever price they will fetch, there was a state-controlled economy. Prices and wages were fixed by the state, and resources – labour, capital and raw materials – were allocated as the state saw fit. In Marxist terms, the communist-ruled states were said to have achieved 'socialism'.

Revolutionary soldiers march through the streets of Moscow during the Russian Revolution of 1917, which brought a communist government to power.

Marx had expected revolutions to take place in the most advanced industrialised countries, where there were the most industrial workers. But the majority of places in which communists actually came to power – including the Soviet Union – were largely agricultural countries with underdeveloped economies and poor-quality government. Communist states struggled to develop their economies, with an emphasis on expanding their industries. In this, to begin with, they were often quite successful.

However, the combination of single-party rule and a state-run economy proved to be very far from a 'workers' paradise'. It certainly did not give working people control over their own lives. Despite believing in the eventual 'withering away' of the state, communists created states with immense power over the individual. Citizens had no right to vote for an alternative government if they did not like the one in power, nor did they generally even have the right to protest or argue against the regime (system of government). Communist governments frequently used the power of the state ruthlessly to crush real or supposed enemies of the system and to control the population. At times, the communist system of government degenerated into personal dictatorship.

The dream turns sour

Communists often argued that the goal of building socialism and, eventually, a communist world justified the ruthless use of force. By the 1980s, however, it was evident that socialist economies were far from

In the 1990s monuments like this still celebrated communist rule in North Korea. In every communist country, however, governments were under pressure to reform.

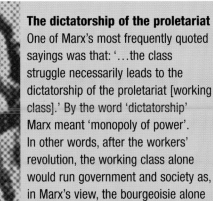

The dictatorship of the proletariat
One of Marx's most frequently quoted sayings was that: '…the class struggle necessarily leads to the dictatorship of the proletariat [working class].' By the word 'dictatorship' Marx meant 'monopoly of power'. In other words, after the workers' revolution, the working class alone would run government and society as, in Marx's view, the bourgeoisie alone ran government and society in a capitalist state.

But Marx's words were clearly open to a different interpretation. Russian revolutionary leader Vladimir Ilyich Lenin wrote: 'The scientific term dictatorship means nothing more or less than authority… absolutely unrestricted by any rules whatever, and based directly on force.' In Lenin's view, Marx's 'dictatorship of the proletariat' meant abandoning all restrictions on the power of the state. This became a feature of communist systems of government.

의 모든 승리의 조직자이며 향도자인 조선로동당 만세!

unleashing the full productive potential of labour and machinery, as Marx had imagined. Instead, communist states were falling disastrously behind the economic growth of free market capitalist economies. This led to desperate attempts at the political and economic reform of communist systems.

The central point of communist rule, as originally conceived, was to end the free market and bring the economy under state control (*see pages 30–31*). But in the 1980s China and the Soviet Union, the two largest communist-ruled countries, accepted that only relaxing state control and introducing a free market could make their economies work. Marxist economics were abandoned. In the Soviet Union and other countries of the 'Soviet bloc' in Eastern Europe, attempts at reform were swiftly followed by the complete collapse of the communist system. In China, single-party communist rule continued, but presiding over an increasingly capitalist economy.

Although the pursuit of an ideal communist society has proved an illusion, the communist system of government remains a practical way of ruling a country. Even in the Soviet Union, it held together through more than seventy difficult years. As long as the Communist Party retains power in China, governing about one-fifth of the world's population, the communist system will be an important part of the world political scene.

As recently as the 1980s, about one in three of the world's population lived in countries with a communist political system. From around 1987 onwards, however, communist systems suffered severe setbacks. Across the world, from central Europe to Asiatic Russia, communist political and economic systems collapsed. By 2004, China was the only major country ruled by a communist party.

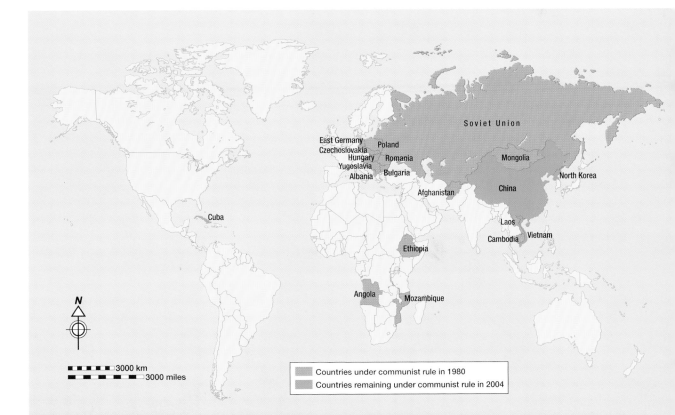

N

3000 km
3000 miles

Countries under communist rule in 1980
Countries remaining under communist rule in 2004

CHAPTER 2

The Rise of Communism

The first communist state was founded in the former Russian Empire by the Bolshevik Party led by Vladimir Ilyich Lenin after a revolution in 1917. The Russian Empire was a vast expanse of Europe and Asia stretching from the Pacific in the east to the Baltic in the west. It was ruled by an emperor, or tsar. In the early 1900s there was much popular discontent in Russia, mainly because of the extreme contrast in wealth between a rich minority and the poverty-stricken majority of the people. Industries were developing rapidly in the early 1900s, but the population of the Russian Empire still consisted mainly of peasants working the land.

Under the oppressive tsarist regime, workers' movements were mostly illegal and Marxist revolutionary activity had to be carried out in secret. Lenin had consequently made the Bolsheviks into a disciplined, secretive body of 'professional revolutionaries'. In 1917 these professional revolutionaries seized power in Russia.

The Bolsheviks played no part in bringing down the Russian Empire. It largely collapsed under the strain of fighting the First World War (1914–18). After a popular uprising against the tsar and the war in the Russian capital Petrograd (St Petersburg), the tsar abdicated in March 1917, and a

> **Communism equals Soviet power plus the electrification of the whole country.**
>
> *The words of Vladimir Illyich Lenin who, along with the other revolutionary leaders in the Soviet Union, was in favour of industrialisation and technological progress, such as the introduction of electric power. They believed that advances in these areas were essential to the communist project.*

Lenin makes a speech in Red Square, Moscow, in November 1918, a year after taking power in Russia.

Provisional Government of liberals and moderate socialists took over. But the government's authority was challenged by 'soviets' – revolutionary committees elected by workers and soldiers. The Bolsheviks were strongly represented in the soviets. They won popular support by promising food for undernourished city-dwellers, an end to the war, and the distribution of land to the peasants. Their slogan was 'Bread, Peace and Land'. In November 1917, Bolshevik workers, soldiers and sailors in Petrograd drove out the Provisional Government. Lenin proclaimed himself head of a revolutionary government.

The Bolshevik regime's chance of surviving at first looked slim. Various groups opposed to the revolution – known collectively as the 'Whites' in contrast to the Bolshevik 'Reds' – formed armies which controlled much of the territory of the former Russian Empire. With the backing of foreign powers, including Britain and France, they attacked the areas under Bolshevik control, starting a civil war that lasted until 1921. Led by Lenin's revolutionary colleague Leon Trotsky, the Bolshevik Red Army eventually triumphed over the White armies.

Power struggles

The Bolsheviks were also opposed by other revolutionary parties, which wanted to share in power. The Bolshevik Party had considerable support among Russia's industrial workers, but had almost no following among the peasants, who made up the majority of the population. When a democratically elected Constituent Assembly met in January 1918, the Bolsheviks had only about a quarter of the seats. The assembly was immediately closed down. With absolute ruthlessness, Lenin used his secret police to crush rival revolutionary parties. He did not stop short of attacking the working class, on whose behalf the revolution was supposedly being conducted. In 1921, when revolutionary sailors at Kronstadt, near Petrograd, demanded an end to the Bolshevik monopoly of power, Lenin sent troops to put down their mutiny by force.

The early years of the Bolshevik regime were a terrible time in the territories of the former Russian Empire. Apart from the atrocities committed on a

A poster designed in 1920 calls for volunteers to fight in the Red Army, defending the Bolshevik regime in the Russian civil war.

VLADIMIR ILYICH LENIN

Lenin's original name was Vladimir Ilyich Ulyanov. He was born in Simbirsk, Russia, in 1870. His eldest brother, Alexander Ulyanov, was hanged in 1887 for plotting to assassinate Tsar Alexander III. From that time onward, Lenin devoted his entire existence to the cause of Marxist revolution. He was arrested for his subversive political activities in 1895 and sent as a prisoner to Siberia for three years. In 1903, when the Russian Social Democratic Labour Party split in two, Lenin led the more radical Bolshevik faction. He was living in exile in Switzerland when the Russian Revolution erupted in March 1917. Returning to Russia, he led the Bolsheviks to seize power the following November. His uncompromising leadership helped the revolutionary regime survive the difficult period of civil war from 1918–21, but at the expense of crushing all political freedom. He survived an assassination attempt by a revolutionary opposed to the Bolshevik monopoly of power in 1918, but the injuries he suffered undermined his health. He died in 1924. After his death his body was embalmed (preserved) and placed on display in a mausoleum in Red Square, Moscow, which became a place of pilgrimage for Soviet citizens.

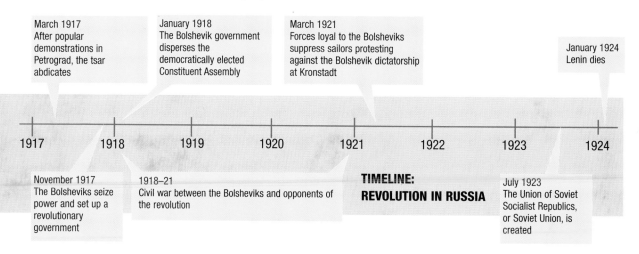

March 1917
After popular demonstrations in Petrograd, the tsar abdicates

January 1918
The Bolshevik government disperses the democratically elected Constituent Assembly

March 1921
Forces loyal to the Bolsheviks suppress sailors protesting against the Bolshevik dictatorship at Kronstadt

January 1924
Lenin dies

1917 1918 1919 1920 1921 1922 1923 1924

November 1917
The Bolsheviks seize power and set up a revolutionary government

1918–21
Civil war between the Bolsheviks and opponents of the revolution

July 1923
The Union of Soviet Socialist Republics, or Soviet Union, is created

large scale by both Red and White armies, there was famine and terrible poverty. But Lenin's regime clung on to power, not only in Russia but through most of the territory of the former Russian Empire. In 1923, the Union of Soviet Socialist Republics (USSR or Soviet Union) was officially founded, ruled by the Bolshevik Party, now renamed the Communist Party of the Soviet Union.

Until the Bolshevik revolution in Russia, Marxists had always assumed that the workers' revolution would start in one of the world's most economically advanced nations. Countries with the most industrial development had the most factory workers, and these were the people who were supposedly the natural supporters of the revolution. Even Lenin at first believed that a revolutionary regime in Russia could not survive unless there were revolutions elsewhere to give it support. In 1918, Germany – in political chaos after defeat in the First World War – looked ripe for a communist seizure of power, but an uprising in Berlin in early 1919 was suppressed and its leaders, Rosa Luxemburg and Karl Liebknecht, were murdered. Shortlived communist governments in Bavaria and in Hungary were crushed in 1919. This left the communists in Moscow (the Russian capital from 1918) isolated.

German communist Rosa Luxemburg addresses a crowd in Stuttgart immediately before the First World War. Luxemburg was murdered during a failed revolutionary uprising in Berlin in 1919.

The socialist movement fragments

In 1919, the Third International, or Comintern, was created as a Moscow-based international organisation to promote revolution worldwide. In almost every country, the socialist movement was divided in two, as communist parties adhering to Comintern split from social democrat parties that rejected the call to world revolution and sought to achieve power through winning votes in elections. In practice, all communist parties soon came to a large degree under the control of Moscow, since they accepted that their first duty was to ensure the survival of the Soviet Union, the world's only revolutionary state.

Lenin died in 1924, shortly after the creation of the Soviet Union. There followed a fierce power struggle within the party leadership. Lenin's most obvious potential successor was the brilliant intellectual Trotsky. But it was Joseph Stalin who came out on top, using his control over the party to defeat his opponents.

Stalinism

By 1929, Stalin had a firm grip on power. But there were huge issues to be resolved about the direction that the revolution should take. In external affairs, there was the question of how committed the Soviet Union was to world revolution. Stalin stood for building 'socialism in a single country' and putting world revolution on the back burner. In internal affairs, economic policy was the most important issue. In an effort to rebuild the country's ruined economy after the civil war, Lenin had introduced the New Economic Policy (NEP), which allowed a limited amount of capitalist free enterprise. In particular, the peasants were encouraged to increase food production on the land they had acquired in the revolution by being permitted to sell their products for profit in a free market. Stalin, along with most other leading Soviet communists, believed that this mild return to capitalism could not be tolerated any longer when the government's main aim was to build a socialist society.

TROTSKY

Lev Davidovich Bronstein was born in Yanovka, Ukraine – then part of the Russian Empire – in 1879. Arrested in 1898 for revolutionary activity and sent to Siberia, he escaped abroad, taking the name Trotsky. He returned to Russia to lead the St Petersburg soviet (revolutionary workers' committee) during a failed uprising in 1905. He played a role second only to that of Lenin in the Bolshevik seizure of power in 1917, and led the Red Army to victory in the civil war of 1918–21. Trotsky was defeated by Joseph Stalin in the power struggle that followed Lenin's death in 1924 and was expelled from the Soviet Union in 1929. From exile he bitterly criticised Stalin's rule, setting up his own international socialist organisation, the Fourth International. In 1940, he was assassinated by one of Stalin's agents in Mexico.

Joseph Stalin (far right) and Leon Trotsky (second from left) stand together as comrades in 1917 during the early days of the Russian Revolution. They later became bitter enemies.

Collectivisation

Under Stalin's rule from 1929, the Soviet Union embarked on a headlong pursuit of economic and social change. Soviet agriculture was 'collectivised'. Peasants were deprived of their land and forced to become workers on large-scale collective farms. At the same time, a series of state 'plans' was adopted setting targets for breakneck growth in industrial production. Rapid industrialisation was intended both to make the Soviet Union powerful enough to defeat its foreign enemies and to create the basis for a socialist society – enough industrial workers to back a workers' state.

The collectivisation of agriculture in the early 1930s has been described as a war against the Russian peasants. The government had to use armed force to break the peasants' resistance. Millions were arrested and sent to work as slave labourers in prison camps. In the Ukrainian countryside there was mass starvation, as the army seized supplies and took them to feed workers in the cities. In industry, the effect of state planning was often chaotic. The authorities set impossible production targets and blamed failure to achieve them on 'sabotage' – which led to arrests of the alleged saboteurs.

Yet rapid industrial growth did occur – a fact that greatly impressed many people outside the Soviet Union, especially since the rest of the world was at that time plunged in the Great Depression, with high unemployment and stagnant or falling industrial production. In the 1930s, Moscow was the world's fastest growing city.

A Soviet propaganda photo from 1941 illustrates the happiness of women workers on a collective farm.

❝ Had I been ordered to die for the party, not once but three times... I would have obeyed without a moment's hesitation. I had not a slightest doubt that the party line was right. ❞

Eugenia Ginzburg, a young communist who, like millions of other party members, was later sent to a 'Gulag' prison camp, writes about her attitude to the Communist Party in the mid-1930s. Despite the brutality of Stalin's rule, the Communist Party in the Soviet Union inspired the trust and devotion of many Soviet citizens.

Iron fist in an iron glove

Under Stalin's rule, the communist system became a personal dictatorship. State propaganda built up a cult around Stalin as the 'great leader'. All potential rivals for power were crushed. In the 1920s no political activity or expression of opinion outside the party had been allowed, but inside the party there had been open debate on key issues. Under Stalin, that margin of freedom disappeared. After 1934, the secret police were given total power to carry out a reign of terror. The Communist Party was 'purged' of Stalin's opponents. Leading party members – including almost all the Bolshevik leaders who had taken part in the seizure of power in 1917 – were arrested, tortured, subjected to 'show trials' in which they admitted to fantastic charges of treason and sabotage, and then executed. In 1937, it was the turn of the Red Army. Stalin had almost all its senior officers arrested and shot. Millions of ordinary Soviet citizens were sentenced to many years in labour camps for offences that were trivial or totally imaginary.

The situation of the Soviet Union, and the international communist movement, was transformed by the impact of the Second World War (1939–45). Invaded by Nazi Germany in 1941, the Soviet Union suffered appalling losses but eventually emerged triumphant. The Red Army ended the war in control of all of Eastern Europe and a large part of Germany. In the

European countries occupied by Soviet troops at the end of the Second World War later became allies of the Soviet Union, as shown in the map below.

STALIN

Joseph Stalin was born as Iosif Vissarionovich Dzhugashvili in Georgia – then part of the Russian Empire – in 1879. He was twice transported to Siberia (in 1902 and 1913) as punishment for taking part in revolutionary activity inside tsarist Russia. He played a solid, but not outstanding, role in the Bolshevik seizure of power in 1917 and the subsequent civil war. By the time of Lenin's death in 1924, however, he had learned how to manipulate the internal workings of the Communist Party so as to fill key posts with his own supporters. By 1929 he had ousted his main rivals to emerge as unchallenged ruler of the Soviet Union. From the 1930s to his death in 1953, the brutality and paranoia of Stalin's dictatorial regime caused the deaths of millions of people who were executed or sent to prison camps. His victims included all the leaders of the 1917 revolution. Stalin's ruthless style of government enabled him to lead his country to victory in war against Nazi Germany (1941–45) and later to extend Soviet power over all of Eastern Europe.

Countries that became part of the Soviet bloc following the Second World War

Soviet Union

East Germany Poland
Czechoslovakia
Hungary Romania
Bulgaria

N

3000 km
3000 miles

immediate postwar years, communist systems were installed throughout this area – in Poland, Czechoslovakia, Hungary, Romania, Bulgaria and East Germany. Communists also came to power in Yugoslavia and Albania, and at the eastern extremity of the Soviet Union, in North Korea. But the largest expansion of communist rule came in 1949 when guerrilla forces led by Mao Zedong triumphed in a civil war in China.

The government systems set up in these different countries were largely modelled on the example of the Soviet Union. Although in some countries – Poland, for example – parties other than the Communist Party were allowed to function, they were all in practice single-party states (*see Chapter 3*). In all places where communists came to power, large numbers of 'class enemies' of the regime were killed or imprisoned – in China an estimated one million landowners were killed in the first phase of communist rule. Businesses and land were largely or entirely taken from private ownership into state ownership. The secret police had unlimited power to arrest and even execute anyone who dared oppose state policies.

A new direction

With the death of Stalin in 1953, a new phase began in the history of the Soviet Union. After a period of jostling for power, Nikita Khrushchev emerged as Soviet leader. At a party congress in 1956, Khrushchev denounced some of Stalin's crimes and criticised his 'cult of the personality'. The power of the secret police was restricted and

Chinese communist leader Mao Zedong stands on a balcony overlooking Tiananmen Square in Beijing during a mass rally in the 1960s.

MAO ZEDONG

Born the son of a farmer in rural China in 1893, Mao was a founder member of the Chinese Communist Party in 1921. He developed the idea of basing a Marxist revolution on the support of peasants rather than industrial workers, establishing a communist 'soviet' at Jiangxi in rural south-east China in 1931. In 1934 he was driven from Jiangxi by Chinese Nationalist forces, but after the 'Long March' he was able to establish a new power base in north-west China. After the Second World War ended in 1945, he led his guerrilla forces in a civil war, which drove the Nationalists out of mainland China. In 1949 Mao took power in Beijing as chairman of the Communist Party and head of government. His desire to maintain revolutionary enthusiasm led to the unwise policies of the Great Leap Forward in 1958 and the Cultural Revolution of 1966 (*see page 18*), both of which caused immense disruption and loss of life. Mao died in 1976 after a long illness. Since his death many of his policies have been heavily criticised by subsequent Chinese communist leaders.

millions of people were released from prison camps. The same pattern was followed in the Soviet 'satellite states' in Eastern Europe. People were not allowed to challenge the communist system – an attempt by workers in Hungary to overthrow communist rule in 1956 was crushed by Soviet tanks — but as long as they made no trouble, they no longer had to fear arbitrary imprisonment.

Through the 1950s and 1960s the Soviet Union quietly abandoned revolutionary enthusiasm. Khrushchev stated his belief that the communists would one day 'bury' capitalism, but he thought they would do so by proving theirs to be the more technologically and economically efficient system (exactly the reverse of what in the end actually occurred). After Khrushchev fell from power in 1964, his successors, Alexei Kosygin and Leonid Brezhnev, followed an even more conservative line. They were no longer committed to the revolutionary transformation of the Soviet Union – let alone of the world – but thought in terms of improving living standards, guaranteeing national security, and ensuring political stability.

China, however, took a quite different line. In the late 1950s, the Chinese communists denounced Khrushchev's policies as 'revisionist' – an abandonment of true Marxist revolutionary

Soviet tanks roll through the streets of Budapest, Hungary, in 1956. They suppressed an anti-communist uprising.

principles. In 1958, Mao launched the Great Leap Forward, a massively ambitious attempt to expand industrial and agricultural production through harnessing the revolutionary enthusiasm of the Chinese people. Vast communes were created overnight, where people were supposed to lead a collective life – for example, eating all their meals in canteens. But the Great Leap Forward resulted in economic catastrophe and mass starvation. The project was halted in 1959.

The Cultural Revolution

Undeterred, Mao launched an even greater upheaval in Chinese society in 1966 in the Cultural Revolution. Young students – the Red Guards – were encouraged to attack all authority figures identified as 'bourgeois reactionaries'. Teachers, university professors, factory managers and civil servants were singled out for punishment. Millions of people considered insufficiently revolutionary were sent to the countryside for 're-education' through manual labour. Once again there was chaos and many deaths before a degree of order began to return in the late 1960s.

The Cold War

The USA and its allies viewed the expansion of the area of the world under communist rule after 1945 with fear and hostility. From 1947, the USA undertook to aid any country that felt threatened by 'communist aggression'. An armed confrontation between the Soviet bloc and the USA and its West European allies started in the late 1940s and lasted for forty years. It became known as the Cold War.

US President John F. Kennedy (in car, wearing sunglasses) visits a US Army missile headquarters in 1962. During the Cold War such missiles were constantly ready for use against the Soviet Union.

Both sides accumulated massive arsenals of nuclear weapons, although a Third World War was avoided. There were, however, major local conflicts – the Korean War (1950–53) and the Vietnam War (c.1964–1975) – in which the USA tried to hold the line against communism.

Nevertheless, the number of countries with some form of communist system of government continued to increase. Marxism had great appeal for many people in the developing world, who saw themselves as victims of capitalist exploitation by the rich 'imperialist' countries of Western Europe and North America. The Soviet Union and China offered practical examples of forms of government and economic development that could be independent of world capitalism. Established communist states – especially the Soviet Union – were also ready to provide military and financial aid to countries that declared in favour of communism. Countries in the developing world that adopted some form of communist system from the 1950s to the 1970s included Cuba, Vietnam, Cambodia, Afghanistan, Ethiopia, and Angola. Communists could still believe that theirs was the way of the future.

"Every year, humanity takes a step towards communism. Maybe not you, but at all events your grandson will surely be a communist."

Soviet leader Nikita Khrushchev, speaking to a British diplomat in 1956.

Young men enrol in the militia of the communist MPLA (Popular Movement for the Liberation of Angola) government in Angola in 1975. The MPLA took power in Angola in that year, when the country won its independence from Portuguese rule. The MPLA immediately faced attacks by troops from white-ruled South Africa and by other Angolan groups backed by the USA. Cuban leader Fidel Castro sent troops to support the MPLA.

CHAPTER 3

Running a Communist State

Communist political systems are often difficult to describe because the way they work in practice may have little to do with how they are really supposed to work. Although communist states have written constitutions setting out every detail of the government system, the reality of government may be quite different. For example, the most powerful figure in a communist country may have an official post that is neither that of head of state nor head of government. Joseph Stalin ruled the Soviet Union for a quarter of a century as general secretary of the Communist Party. From 1959, Mao Zedong ceased to be head of the Chinese government, yet still exercised supreme power as the chairman of the Communist Party's chief policy-making committee, the Politburo. In an extreme case, Deng Xiaoping was recognised as 'paramount leader' of China up to 1997, although he had resigned from all official posts ten years earlier.

The single-party system

The government structure of communist states has not been strikingly different from that of non-communist countries. Although in 1917 the Bolsheviks rejected the idea of having 'ministers' to head government departments, instead calling members of the government 'people's commissars', this was abandoned in 1946. The Soviet Union then had a president, prime minister, foreign minister, and so on, like most Western European countries. Similarly, in other communist states governments were formed on familiar lines, with departments headed by ministers and a state bureaucracy, created to put the measures determined by government departments into effect.

The distinguishing feature of communist systems, however, has been the dominant role of the Communist Party. In the Chinese constitution, for example, the Chinese Communist Party is described as 'the sole political party in power' and 'the leader of the Chinese people'. In a fully developed

The Chinese parliament, the National People's Congress (NPC), meets at the Great Hall of the People in Beijing in 2004. The NPC's 3,000 delegates, drawn from all parts of China, have little real power, and they generally approve without question policies put forward by the ruling Communist Party.

THE HENLEY COLLEGE LIBRARY

HOW GOVERNMENT WORKS IN CHINA

PARTY

**Standing Committee of
the Politburo**

⬆

Political Bureau (Politburo)

⬆

Central Committee

⬆

National Party Congress

STATE

President

⬆

State Council

⬆

**National People's
Congress (NPC)**

communist system, the party controls every element of society: the government and the civil service; the armed forces, police and judiciary; trade unions, farms and factories; the media and education; sport and culture. The government and its bureaucracy both operate entirely under the party's direction.

In communist states the ruling parties form parallel structures to the state organisation – the party has its own leadership, bureaucracy and 'parliament'. Typically, local party committees elect delegates to Party Congresses. The Party Congress elects a Central Committee, which in turn elects the Political Bureau (Politburo) and the Secretariat. It is within these party structures, not the government, that real power is exercised and political issues are decided. Similarly only those with the right credentials and party loyalty can become officials and leaders in society.

In principle, communist systems are democracies in which all citizens, except some vaguely defined as 'enemies of the people', have the right to vote. However, no communist regime has ever tolerated significant political activity outside the Communist Party. As a result, there have been no alternative parties or candidates for

All communist government systems have roughly parallel organs of party and state. In China, power officially lies with an elected National People's Congress, which in turn elects the State Council and the country's president. In practice, however, most power lies with the Communist Party's Politburo and, above all, the few leaders that make up the Politburo's Standing Committee. Many leading figures hold top positions both in the party and the state.

21

voters to choose between. Typically, a single candidate approved by Communist Party committees stands for election. After the voting, the candidate is declared to have received 99 or even 100 per cent of the vote.

With political debate and democracy outside the Communist Party blocked, the degree of free discussion and democracy within the ruling party has been a crucial issue in communist states. For example, in the Soviet Union during the first few years after the 1917 Bolshevik seizure of power, opposing groups organised within the party to campaign for alternative polices, hoping to win crucial votes in the Party Congress or Central Committee. But Lenin disapproved of such 'factions', which he believed undermined party unity and discipline.

Repression of differences

By the time the Soviet Union was founded in 1923, organised factions within the party had been banned. Vigorous discussion of issues went on in the party for a few more years, but with the rise to power of Joseph Stalin this also stopped. Stalin perfected the technique of controlling who was put forward for election at each level of the party, so that only those prepared to support him unquestioningly were elected. By the mid-1930s, any party member even suspected of

Members of the Politburo of the Soviet Communist Party, including party leader Mikhail Gorbachev (bottom right), vote to remove Andrei Gromyko (bottom centre) as Soviet president in 1988. Such unanimous votes discredited the Soviet system.

" **Today we do not even know the height or size of a person we elect, let alone his character or ability. We have simply become ballot-casting machines.** "

In 1957, the communist regime in China briefly allowed a measure of freedom of expression, following Mao's slogan: 'Let a hundred flowers bloom'. This liberal impulse resulted in a torrent of criticism of the regime. The above quotation is by an anonymous critic who wrote of the way elections were conducted.

holding views differing from the official party line –
as laid down by Stalin and his followers – would face
arrest and possible execution.

Stalinist repression of all differences within the
ruling party has existed in different communist states
at various times – in the early twenty-first century,
North Korea is still run along Stalinist lines. But there
have also been periods of relative openness in
communist parties. In China since the 1980s, for
example, the ruling party has hotly debated the
direction of political and economic policies. Party
leaders of differing views have sought support for their
conflicting positions. Even at their most open, however,
decision-making in communist states has remained
something that happens away from the public eye.
A communist leadership never loses a vote in the
Central Committee or Party Congress, nor are issues
ever decided there in open debate. The debates always
have clear limits, and all party members know they
must not directly attack the party leadership or policies
that are regarded as the essential 'party line'.

*In 1966, during the Chinese Cultural Revolution, students and
teachers parade through Beijing holding placards in praise of
Chairman Mao Zedong.*

Party membership and privileges
In all communist states, only a
minority of the population has
belonged to the party. For example, the
Chinese Communist Party has around
50 million members, about 4 per cent
of the total population. Party members
have tended to include all those in
senior positions of authority.
Possession of a party membership
card has been a ticket to privilege,
giving access to better housing,
holidays, healthcare and education.

In the Soviet Union, special shops
catered only for party members,
selling goods not available to the
general population. The threat of
being expelled from the party has
always been a serious one, involving
not only losing these privileges but
also almost certainly losing your job
as well. So party members have had
a strong reason not to rock the boat –
to observe party discipline and strictly
follow the party line.

The emphasis on party discipline and unity means that communist states have no system for removing current leaders from power and replacing them with new ones. As a result, communist leaders once in place have tended to stay in power until they die of old age. Even then, it is often difficult arranging who is to succeed them. In some countries, where the communist system evolved into a personal dictatorship, the hereditary principle has emerged as a solution. In North Korea, the country's first communist leader, Kim Il-Sung, ruled for forty-five years, and then was succeeded by his son, Kim Jong-Il. Nicolae Ceauçescu, leader of communist Romania for a quarter of a century, was intending to have his son succeed him, a plan never put into effect because of the fall of communism in Eastern Europe in 1989.

In Romania, soldiers and demonstrators celebrate the downfall of communist leader Nicolae Ceauçescu in December 1989. Ceauçescu had turned Romania's communist regime into a corrupt personal dictatorship.

Political manoeuvring

Most commonly, however, a change of leadership or a succession is decided by a power struggle behind closed doors. On occasions these power struggles have been brutal affairs, as in the case of the fall of the Gang of Four in China (*see panel opposite*) in 1976. But mostly they have been carried out in a relatively civilised and orderly manner, by political manoeuvring among party leaders. Khrushchev, for example, was removed as leader of the Soviet Communist Party in 1964 when the rest of the party leadership combined against him while he was away on holiday. A meeting of the Central Committee was hastily convened to approve the decision with a vote, and Khrushchev went peacefully into retirement. To take another example, a new generation of leaders came to the forefront in China in the 1990s without any upheaval or disruption.

Participation of the masses

Politics of the kind found in liberal democracies – campaigning by political parties offering alternative policies, elections that will decide who runs the government – does not exist in communist states. Nevertheless communist states have often required a high level of political participation from their citizens. In their most actively 'revolutionary' phases, they have devoted considerable energy to mobilising and indoctrinating 'the masses'. At the time of Mao's leadership (*see page 16*) in China, for example, peasants and workers had to spend breaks from work reading and discussing the thoughts of Chairman Mao Zedong, published in the *Little Red Book*.

Even at times when revolutionary enthusiasm has been less intense, local party committees or party officials in workplaces have made sure that the party line is known to and followed by non-party members.

Left: The Little Red Book *– compulsory reading for Chinese citizens in the time of Mao Zedong.*

Below: The Gang of Four, from left: Zhang Chunqiao, Wang Hongwen, Yao Wenyuan and Jiang Qing.

The fall of the Gang of Four

On 9 September 1976, Mao Zedong died after a long illness. The leadership struggle that followed was brief and brutal. Mao's widow Jiang Qing, backed by three other radical members of the Politburo – Zhang Chunqiao, Yao Wenyuan and Wang Hongwen – claimed the right to succeed Mao. They were all associated with the extremist policies of the Cultural Revolution.

They were resisted by Hua Guofeng, a member of the leadership who had come under attack during the Cultural Revolution and who had recently been appointed China's prime minister. Hua had the support of key military forces in Beijing. On 6 October 1976, he had the four radicals arrested. Branded 'the Gang of Four', they were charged with a host of crimes, from stirring up civil war and undermining the education system to importing expensive stereo equipment and secretly watching *The Sound of Music* (a banned foreign film)! All received lengthy prison sentences. Hua succeeded Mao as party chairman – although he was soon himself elbowed aside by Deng Xiaoping.

They have made it more or less compulsory for workers to take part in meetings or demonstrations in support of the party leaders or specific party policies, cast a vote for the sole candidate in an election, or join a party youth organisation.

In theory, in a fully developed communist system there are no independent organisations or centres of power. Party discipline should ensure that everyone follows the same party line. So in the Soviet Union, for example, although there were national 'republics' – Ukraine, Byelorus, Georgia, and so on – that had their own governments, they were all run by Communist Party members and so could not be centres of opposition or diversity. To take another example, in a communist system, trade unions are party-run organisations. As a result, they serve to mobilise the workers in line with state and party policy, not to represent the interests of workers in opposition to the state.

Abuses of power

This 'monolithic', or unshakeable image deliberately presented by communist states has generally been a front more than a reality. Party politicians have been able to build up independent power bases in the governments of cities or regions. The secret police and the army, although led by party members, have been powerful forces to be reckoned with, often pursuing their own interests. In China, for example, the People's Liberation Army took the initiative in ending the Cultural Revolution in the 1960s because senior officers objected to the disorder it caused. Senior bureaucrats have also often been able to operate in their own sphere with little reference to central authority.

Even if communist systems are less monolithic than they might pretend, they have given little place to the freedom of the individual. Marxists criticised liberal democracies for their 'dishonest' way of representing the rule of law and freedom of speech. Such rules and freedoms, Marxists argued, merely disguised the oppression of the working class by the capitalists. This attitude encouraged Marxists once in power themselves to ignore the need for individual freedom and proper legal process. Communist states have in theory accorded equal rights to all citizens (apart from loosely defined 'class enemies') but this has at times meant virtually no rights for anyone.

Dissidents
From the 1960s to the 1980s in the Soviet Union, individual Soviet 'dissidents' bravely challenged the lack of freedom in their country, publicising human rights abuses and spreading ideas critical of the regime. Notable dissidents included the novelist Aleksandr Solzhenitsyn and the prominent nuclear physicist Andrei Sakharov. Denounced by the Soviet authorities as 'isolated renegades', they were harassed and persecuted for their views. Solzhenitsyn was deported to Western Europe in 1974, while in 1980 Sakharov was sent into 'internal exile' in the city of Gorky, where he was largely cut off from communication with the outside world. Sakharov was released in 1986 when a new Soviet leader, Mikhail Gorbachev, began his attempt to liberalise the Soviet regime.

❝ Everyone here is scared – the youth, even more the elderly. That is precisely why our technology is so far behind. ❞

In these words, spoken in the 1970s, the veteran Chinese communist leader Deng Xiaoping recognised the link between achieving technological progress and the need to free citizens from the fear that speaking their minds openly might lead to imprisonment (or worse) by the authorities.

A government poster in China encourages parents to restrict their family to a single child. This campaign reflects China's emphasis on the needs of society over the goal of individual freedom.

Lack of individual freedom

In practice, such matters as the degree of freedom of expression, and the respect accorded to individuals or groups with specific non-communist beliefs (for example, believers in various religions), have varied in different communist systems at different times. The Soviet Union and China brutally persecuted non-communist intellectuals and religious believers, but in more relaxed times they broadly tolerated diversity that did not directly threaten the system. No communist state, however, has effectively guaranteed respect for individual freedoms. Marxists have argued that social values should come before individual values, and that communist systems grant social and economic rights, such as rights to basic welfare or employment, that capitalist democracies fail to provide.

Whatever the rights or wrongs of this argument, communist systems have proved to have serious drawbacks. The absence of free criticism of those in authority, and of democratic means for removing them, has tended to lead to abuse of power and corruption. With the state in control of economic life, the lack of a free market has led to gross inefficiency. For example, consumer goods such as washing machines were often of very poor quality because the people who made them did not stand to make a profit if they sold more, so could not care less whether customers were satisfied or not. The failings of communist systems were painfully exposed when reforms were attempted in the 1980s.

CHAPTER 4
Life Under Communism

At its most extreme, life under communist regimes has been, for some groups of people, a living hell. This was true for peasants in the Ukraine, subjected to Stalin's policy of collectivising Soviet agriculture in the 1930s. It was true for city dwellers in Phnom Penh, Cambodia, driven out into the 'killing fields' by Khmer Rouge revolutionaries in 1975 (*see panel*). In any discussion of communism, it must never be forgotten how, at times, the attempt at a revolutionary transformation of society cost many millions of lives. But outside such periods of extremism and upheaval, life in communist states has generally not been so radically dissimilar to life in capitalist societies of a comparable level of economic development.

The Killing Fields

Cambodia, in south-east Asia, was the site of one of the most determined attempts ever made to create a communist society. After Khmer Rouge guerrillas took power there in 1975, all city dwellers were forced to march out into the country at gunpoint. There they were made to work on collective farms. Communal life was rigorously enforced. For example, all food had to be eaten in canteens, so even picking and eating a wild berry off a bush was severely punished. Hundreds of thousands of people died of disease, exhaustion and mistreatment, or were summarily executed for 'crimes' such as knowing how to speak a foreign language (evidence of relations with foreigners). The Khmer Rouge was overthrown by fellow communists from Vietnam in 1979. Cambodia ceased to be a communist state in 1991.

The remains of thousands of the victims of the killing fields were put on display in Cambodia in the 1980s after the fall of the Khmer Rouge regime.

Experiments in collective living

In principle, communists believed in emphasising the collective life of society instead of the private life of individuals or families, which is stressed by capitalist societies. There have been some notable large-scale experiments with collective living. For example, in rural China from the late 1950s to the 1980s, most peasants lived in 'communes'. Household work, cooking and child-rearing were largely carried out collectively by the commune, rather than by individuals in their family homes. Much of the work on the land was done by large gangs of peasants organised in 'work brigades', rather than by individual peasant farmers. Rations were distributed equally to those who worked. According to the Chinese government, this was 'leading the peasants toward a happier collective life.'

In general, though, the desire for 'collective life' in communist states resulted in little more than the organisation of group holidays by factories for their workers, or the staging of frequent political meetings and demonstrations in which people were virtually forced to take part (as under Stalin in the Soviet Union in the 1930s). Most young people in the Soviet bloc belonged to communist youth organisations, but these were in practice little different from groups such as the scouts or guides in Western societies.

Individual ambition

In the early days of the Soviet Union there was talk of abolishing marriage and bringing up children in state nurseries, but this came to nothing. Individual ambition – the wish to 'get on in life' – flourished, even more within the ruling party than outside it. While official propaganda presented party members as self-sacrificing idealists 'building socialism', in practice the party was the route to power or influence. Ambitious careerists joined the

Chinese children photographed in 1983 wear the red scarves of the Young Pioneers communist youth organisation. Such organisations were often little different from groups such as the scouts or guides in the West. However, the school curriculum in communist countries is strictly controlled to teach the Marxist view of history and society.

Communist Party to guarantee their success. Party members had the most spacious apartments, the best cars, the best schools for their children. In Soviet cities, there were special shops open only to party members where luxury goods were for sale that were simply unavailable in ordinary stores.

Society in communist countries with state-owned economies was consistently more 'egalitarian' (equal) than in capitalist states. Since there were no big businessmen or financiers or large landowners, a class of truly rich people did not exist. But successful individuals in the party bureaucracy, state bureaucracy, secret police and army (all party members) nonetheless constituted a highly privileged élite. They were not rich by Western standards, but their privileges were glaring hypocrisy since they were people who preached equality as an ideal.

Lack of incentive

State-run economic systems, found in all communist countries until the 1980s, proved in the long-term an inefficient way of providing for people's needs. The output per acre from collective farms was significantly lower than when peasants were allowed to farm their own plots for sale in a free market. In industry there were similar productivity problems. The state at times managed to drive workers and managers to raise output by threatening punishments if they fell short of targets, or appealing to their commitment to the revolutionary cause. But in the longer term, lack of free market competition and of the profit motive led to falling output and a poor quality of product – there was simply no incentive to produce more and better goods. In Poland there was a cynical popular saying: 'We pretend to work and they pretend to pay us' – in other words, since the communist state paid its workers so poorly, whether they worked hard or not, the workers put little effort into their jobs.

There were also serious problems with the allocation of economic resources. State plans for the economy consistently focussed on developing heavy industry – iron and steel, coal-mining, or making heavy machinery – rather than 'frivolous' products for everyday use, such as washing machines, televisions or family cars. When communist regimes, worried by their unpopularity, tried to turn to making household

Question: 'When you die, would you rather go to a capitalist hell or a socialist hell?' Answer: 'A socialist hell, of course. You get roasted in the flames of hell in both cases; but in a socialist hell, there is a shortage of matches, they've run out of wood, and the Devil is not working at the moment.'

A joke from communist-ruled East Germany. The inefficiency of socialist society compared with the capitalist West was a source of humour among ordinary people living under communist rule.

consumer goods, they proved to be bad at it. Unresponsive to consumer demand, they were always more likely to decide to produce what they thought people should want, rather than what they really wanted.

Queues and shortages

Communist societies became places of constant queueing. Whereas in a capitalist free market economy products in short supply became expensive, in communist states they remained affordable – because their price was fixed by the state – but almost impossible to obtain. There were shortages of almost everything. People in the cities would carry shopping bags at all times, in case they happened to pass a shop with something worthwhile for sale, immediately recognisable by the queue outside. In a less literal sense, queues existed for everything from decent housing to a family car. You might have to wait years to obtain a car after putting your name down for one – and then it would probably be a vehicle of poor performance, like the infamous East German Trabant. Plain economic inefficiency was probably the most widespread source of the unpopularity of communist governments.

❝ You might for instance hear on the train to work that a load of fresh oranges had just been delivered to a certain store at the other end of town. You had to decide between being on time for work... or being an hour or two late in order to secure a week's supply of oranges. ❞

An East German woman describes the everyday struggle to find items in short supply during the period of communist rule.

In communist East Germany in the 1980s, the Trabant car was cramped, slow and polluting, but it was the best car anyone could hope to own. People put their names on a waiting list for years to get one.

In 1990, Cubans celebrate the thirty-first anniversary of Fidel Castro coming to power. Many people in Cuba respect Castro as a national leader, taking pride in his defiance of Cuba's powerful neighbour, the USA.

Restricted freedoms

Some social groups felt the limitations of freedom more acutely than others. Artists and intellectuals often had a hard time under communist systems, facing the demand that their ideas and creations should follow the party line. Religious believers at times faced harassment or outright oppression, as did members of national or ethnic groups that had for some reason earned the disfavour of the communist state. All of society had to put up with surveillance by the secret police and by police informers.

People took it for granted that you had to be careful what you said, even in private. If you were known to have criticised the authorities, it would at best harm your prospects of promotion at work, or at worst get you into serious trouble. What many people most resented, especially in the Soviet bloc, was the ban on travel to countries outside the communist sphere, which applied to all but the most privileged individuals.

The successes of communism

Yet it would be wrong to give the impression that communist systems were universally unpopular. In the Soviet Union, China, Vietnam and Cuba, communist governments generated intense national

pride through standing up to foreigners in peace and war. Technological achievements such as the space programmes in both the Soviet Union and China also excited genuine patriotic enthusiasm. Communist states invested heavily in sport, with the result that countries such as the Soviet Union, East Germany and Romania often produced outstanding results at the Olympics. The citizens of these countries obviously liked seeing their athletes win.

Communist states also recorded positive achievements in many aspects of social life. They established universal education and literacy, and brought about great improvements in health care. Rents were kept low and the basics of life were affordable for all. People generally had a secure existence, with no risk of unemployment, little stress at work, and a state pension to look forward to in old age. Communist states were also theoretically committed to equal status for women long before this was generally accepted in the capitalist world. Although the position of women varied, they usually benefited from at least some advantages rarely found in non-communist states – for example, access to subsidised nurseries so that mothers with young children could go out to work.

Many people who lived through the transition from communism to capitalism in the Soviet bloc later looked back on at least elements of the communist system with nostalgia, regretting the loss of order and security. On the other hand, the lure of the plentiful consumer goods and the freer lifestyle offered by capitalism was irresistible.

First man in space
On 12 April 1961, Soviet cosmonaut Yuri Gagarin became the first human to travel outside the earth's atmosphere. The Soviet Union's achievement in putting the first man into space won great prestige for communism in general. It seemed to imply that the communist system was overtaking the capitalist world in technological progress and to validate communism's claim to be a superior form of social and economic organisation.

Soviet sprinter Valery Borsov raises his arms in triumph after winning a gold medal in the 200 metres at the Munich Olympic Games in 1972. Communist states were very successful in pushing their athletes to sporting success.

CHAPTER 5

The Decline of Communism

In the 1960s, communist leaders were on the whole still confident that their system was proving the way of the future. From that decade onward, however, communist states began to slip at an accelerating rate into crisis. Their failure to achieve continued economic growth created a worsening gap between the level of development in communist-ruled states and that in much of the capitalist world. Communist leaders increasingly came to believe that their political and economic systems were in need of radical reform. But attempts at reform soon revealed how much popular discontent was simmering beneath the surface within communist countries, just waiting for a chance to erupt.

Eastern Europe

The weakest area of communist rule was always Eastern Europe, occupied by Soviet forces at the end of the Second World War. Although there were national communist parties in East European countries, the regimes in Poland, Hungary, Czechoslovakia, and East Germany ultimately depended on the backing of Soviet military might. Communist rulers in Eastern Europe made concessions in an effort to win popular support. In Poland, for example, small farmers were allowed to keep their land and the influence of the Catholic Church was tolerated within certain limits. But the communist rulers were always identified with the domination of a foreign power – the Soviet Union – and resented by many people who wanted full national independence.

The Prague Spring

The first major attempt at reform from within a communist party came in Czechoslovakia, when Alexander Dubcek became party leader in January 1968. Dubcek abolished censorship and proposed a limited but genuine liberalisation of the economy and political life. His gamble was that, offered

❝ Socialism is whatever brings happiness to the people. ❞

General Vo Nguyen Giap was one of the Vietnamese leaders who fought wars against France and the USA to establish independence from foreign rule and to introduce communism to his country. In 1995, after Vietnam had followed China in abandoning Marxist economic policies, Giap was asked what had happened to his socialist ideals. This quotation was his reply.

Alexander Dubcek tried to liberalise the communist system in Czechoslovakia in 1968.

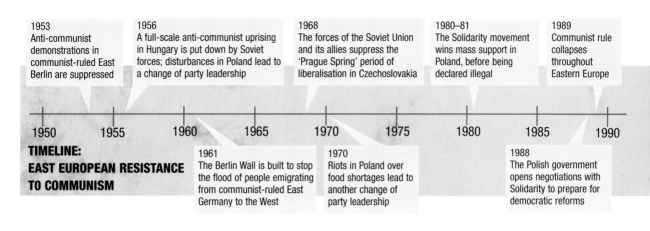

1953
Anti-communist demonstrations in communist-ruled East Berlin are suppressed

1956
A full-scale anti-communist uprising in Hungary is put down by Soviet forces; disturbances in Poland lead to a change of party leadership

1968
The forces of the Soviet Union and its allies suppress the 'Prague Spring' period of liberalisation in Czechoslovakia

1980–81
The Solidarity movement wins mass support in Poland, before being declared illegal

1989
Communist rule collapses throughout Eastern Europe

1950   1955   1960   1965   1970   1975   1980   1985   1990

1961
The Berlin Wall is built to stop the flood of people emigrating from communist-ruled East Germany to the West

1970
Riots in Poland over food shortages lead to another change of party leadership

1988
The Polish government opens negotiations with Solidarity to prepare for democratic reforms

freedom, people would choose to support his liberal version of communism. But in the excitement of the political debate and creative activity that followed liberalisation – a period known as the 'Prague Spring' – it soon became obvious that, given genuine freedom, the people of Czechoslovakia were unlikely to opt for communism at all. In August 1968, the Soviet Union and its allies sent in tanks to suppress Czech freedom and unseat Dubcek, restoring hardline communist rule.

Solidarity

When the next major crisis erupted in Eastern Europe, the Soviet tanks stayed at home. In 1980–81, the Solidarity trade union movement in Poland led by Lech Walesa, shook the communist system to its roots. Starting with a strike at the Lenin shipyard at Gdansk, it developed into a nationwide protest movement demanding freedom and democracy. In December 1981, the authorities declared Solidarity illegal and ordered the arrest of its leaders. The head of the Polish army, General Wojciech Jaruzelski, took over leadership of the state

Supporters of the Polish Solidarity movement attend an open-air Catholic mass in Warsaw in 1982. The Catholic Church provided a focus for opposition to communist rule in Poland.

and the party. Poland was in effect under military rule – a clear indication that the Communist Party no longer had enough popular support to run the country.

The Solidarity movement revealed the lack of popular support for communism, especially among working class people. This was a shock for parties committed to the myth that they represented 'the working masses'. Although nothing was said publicly, even some figures within the leadership of the Soviet Communist Party were acutely aware of stagnation in their society on all fronts. The twin bureaucracies of the party and the state had become systems for providing secure and privileged employment for an often corrupt minority. Meanwhile, industry suffered from low output and high pollution levels. Agricultural production on collective farms was dismally low. Technologically and economically the Soviet Union was falling ever further behind the West. Crucially, it was becoming increasingly difficult to keep up with the USA in the arms race of the Cold War.

Glasnost and perestroika

In 1985, Mikhail Gorbachev became head of the Soviet Communist Party. After a period consolidating his hold on the party machine, in 1987 he launched a radical reform programme. His watchwords were 'glasnost' (openness) and 'perestroika' (restructuring). 'Glasnost' meant allowing freedom of expression and political debate. 'Perestroika' meant above all reforming the inefficient state-run economy, introducing elements of a free market and free enterprise. A convinced communist, Gorbachev believed that his reforms would put communism back on the right track. But his policies led at breakneck speed to the collapse of communist rule in the Soviet bloc.

In Eastern Europe, communist rule was too unpopular to survive once Gorbachev removed the threat of Soviet military intervention to prop it up. Told by the Soviet government to embrace the new 'openness', in 1989 East European communist regimes fell in the face of mass demonstrations calling for freedom, democracy, and full national independence.

MIKHAIL GORBACHEV

Born in 1931, Mikhail Gorbachev joined the Soviet Communist Party at the age of twenty-one. He rose steadily through the party ranks, eventually winning the favourable attention of powerful KGB (secret police) chief Yuri Andropov. In 1978, Andropov had Gorbachev appointed to the powerful party Secretariat and, two years later, to the Politburo, the Soviet Union's top policy-making body.

When Andropov became party leader (general secretary) in 1983, Gorbachev was his right-hand man as efforts began to reform the Soviet economy. These were halted when Andropov died in the following year. In 1985, Gorbachev became general secretary and soon initiated a political liberalisation and economic reform programme. He also sought agreement with the USA to end the Cold War. In 1988 he was elected head of state – president of the USSR – as part of a move away from the concentration of power in the hands of the party. Although committed to keeping the Soviet Union in existence, Gorbachev refused to join in an attempted *coup* (against the Russian Federation president, Boris Yeltsin) by communist hardliners in August 1991 who wanted to restore the power of the Communist Party. The disintegration of the Soviet Union the following December left Gorbachev with no country to rule.

The system collapses

Even at that date, however, few people anticipated the fall of communism in the Soviet Union. Yet both sides of Gorbachev's reform policy went wrong. Rather than solving the Soviet Union's economic problems, 'perestroika' led to chaos, especially in the industrial sector, and a sharp decline in living standards. The new openness of political debate brought a torrent of criticism of communism's past crimes. It also allowed nationalism, previously suppressed in the multinational Soviet Union, to emerge as a major force, with demands for independence from nationalists in some of the Soviet Union's constituent republics.

Former communist Boris Yeltsin was the leader of reformers opposed to Gorbachev. In 1990, Yeltsin won free elections to become president of Russia (Russian Federation), while Gorbachev remained president of the Soviet Union. After facing down a rather half-hearted

At a factory near Moscow in 1987, Soviet leader Mikhail Gorbachev (left) tries to persuade workers to support his reformed brand of communism.

Deng Xiaoping, photographed here in the 1970s, played the leading role in transforming China into a state with a communist government but a largely free market economy.

DENG XIAOPING

Born in China's Sechuan Province in 1904, Deng joined the Communist Party in the 1920s. He took part in the famous 'Long March' in 1934 and the guerrilla war that eventually brought the communists to power in Beijing in 1949. As one of the more conservative and moderate of party leaders, he experienced sharp reversals of fortune. When the Cultural Revolution erupted in 1966, he was driven out of his post as general secretary of the party, publicly humiliated and sent to work in a factory as a form of 're-education'. Restored to a senior position in 1973, he was again dismissed from all posts and subjected to public denunciation in April 1976, accused among other things of intending to restore capitalism.

Remarkably, by 1978 he had not only returned to the party leadership, but had established himself as the dominant figure in the campaign to reform the system and modernise China. In 1987, aged 83, he resigned all official posts, but he continued to be recognised as China's 'paramount leader' until his death in 1997.

attempted *coup* by hardline communists in August 1991, Yeltsin dissolved the Communist Party. At the end of the year, the constituent republics of the USSR agreed to declare themselves independent. As the Soviet Union broke up, Gorbachev was left with nothing to rule. It was a staggeringly casual process. The motherland of communism ceased to exist with hardly a whimper.

Faced with many of the same problems as the Soviet Union, China followed a very different path. The chaotic upheaval of the Cultural Revolution, launched in 1966, was in its way an attempt to reform the communist system. It aimed to shake up the entrenched bureaucracy, not by liberalisation but by re-igniting revolutionary enthusiasm. Its result was, however, further to disrupt China's struggling economy. By the 1970s, the communist leadership was acutely aware their country was falling further behind the West in technological and economic achievement.

The Four Modernisations

The direction that China eventually took was decided by the defeat of the Gang of Four (*see page 25*) and the subsequent rise to power of Deng Xiaoping. A Party Congress held in 1978 approved a new approach based on the 'Four Modernisations' – modernisation of agriculture; industry; national defence; and science and technology. Under Deng's leadership, the state monopoly of the economy was abandoned in favour of a 'socialist market economy'. Peasant farmers, who made up the majority of China's population, were encouraged to grow crops on private plots and sell them for a profit. Foreign capitalists were encouraged to invest in special enterprise zones. Soon China's cities were being transformed by an influx of imported consumer goods, while Chinese factories were providing cheap labour for foreign investors, producing goods for export.

Unlike Gorbachev in the Soviet Union, however, Deng had the Communist Party keep strict control of political life. Protests in favour of freedom of expression and democracy were suppressed in 1976–77, and again even more decisively at Tiananmen Square in 1989. In the cultural sphere there was considerable liberalisation – even if the state still tried to limit such 'subversive' influences as Western films and the Internet. But organised political opposition or serious questioning of communist rule were no more permitted than before. By the twenty-first century, China had what was essentially a free market economy combined with a largely unreformed communist system of government.

Again in contrast to the Soviet Union, China's economic reforms broadly succeeded in their aim. For many Chinese people living standards rose rapidly, and imported technology helped bring about major advances in China's industries. Although huge social problems, including unemployment and mass migration of peasants to the cities arose as a result of the social disruption caused by free market polices, the regime showed no signs of following the Soviet Union into oblivion.

In Beijing's Tiananmen Square, pro-democracy demonstrators and soldiers mingle cheerfully in May 1989. The following month, though, the army crushed the demonstrations.

Tiananmen Square

In the spring of 1989, hundreds of thousands of Chinese people took to the streets to demand Western-style democracy and freedom of expression. The focus of the mass protests became Tiananmen Square in the heart of Beijing, which was permanently occupied by student pro-democracy demonstrators. On 4 June 1989, units of the People's Liberation Army attacked the square, firing on the protesters. Several thousand were killed and thousands more wounded. There were widespread arrests of people connected with the pro-democracy movement, described by the communist media as 'traitors to the people'. The suppression of the Tiananmen Square protests, which shocked world opinion, showed that the Chinese Communist Party had no intention of giving up its monopoly on power.

CHAPTER 6

Communism Present and Future

By the end of the twentieth century, it was commonly said that the 'socialist experiment' had failed. The project to build a new type of society free from exploitation, and in particular the adoption of a state-run economy, had apparently not delivered the goods. The four countries that still have communist government systems in the early twenty-first century – China, North Korea, Cuba and Vietnam – face the future with differing degrees of confidence.

The remaining few

In North Korea, a hardline unreformed communist regime rules with an iron fist over an impoverished land. Individual freedom is non-existent and even the most basic necessities of life are often in short supply, with famine reported in some years. Internationally isolated – China withdrew support in 1995 – North Korea was denounced by the USA as a 'rogue state' in 2001, putting the regime under increasing pressure to reform and to abandon its alleged nuclear weapons programme.

In Cuba, the survival of the communist system seems largely dependent on the personal survival of leader Fidel Castro. The loss of the support of the Soviet Union in 1991 was a serious blow to Cuba, but Castro had defied a hostile USA for three decades and was not prepared to give up or change just because of

Fidel Castro gives a speech in 1989 on the thirtieth anniversary of taking power in Cuba.

FIDEL CASTRO

Cuban leader Fidel Castro was born in 1927, the son of a sugar plantation owner. He worked as a lawyer before getting involved in a failed revolt against Cuban president and US-backed dictator Fulgencio Batista in 1953. Castro fled abroad, but secretly returned to Cuba in 1956. With a small band of armed followers, he started a guerrilla war against Batista's corrupt regime. By 1959 the guerrillas had won control of the country.

Soon after coming to power, Castro declared himself in favour of communism, which brought about a confrontation with the USA. Castro's forces defeated a US-backed invasion by Cuban exiles in 1961. The following year his Soviet allies began to install nuclear missiles in Cuba. The USA demanded the withdrawal of the missiles. The Soviet Union agreed just in time to avoid a war. From that time onward the USA made no serious attempt to overthrow Castro, but continues to subject Cuba to an economic blockade which condemns the country to poverty. When the Soviet Union fell apart in 1991, Cuba lost its only ally, but Castro refused to change his policies.

> **❝ It does not matter whether a cat is black or white; as long as it catches mice it is a good cat. ❞**
>
> *The words of Chinese leader Deng Xiaoping. Deng did not care whether his economic policies were called 'capitalist' or 'socialist'. All he was interested in was whether they worked.*

By the late 1990s, Chinese streets had begun to look like those in any capitalist country, with adverts for imported luxury goods and stylishly dressed passers-by.

events in Moscow. As a result, the collapse of the Soviet Union was followed by the reinforcement of party rule in Cuba – with a tougher crackdown on opponents of the system – and a strengthening of American economic sanctions, designed to bring the regime to its knees.

In Vietnam, communist leaders who had fought against the French and the Americans in turn from the 1940s to the 1970s to secure their country's independence struggled to cope with the legacy of destruction left by decades of warfare. From 1986, they reluctantly abandoned Marxist economics and followed the Soviet Union and China in introducing free market reforms to boost the economy. The result has been rapid economic progress in areas such as tourism and light industry although, as in China, the Communist Party still clings to its monopoly of political power.

Free enterprise in China

China presents a very different picture from the other three communist states. It entered the twenty-first century bursting with confidence and energy. Its communist leaders no longer dream of world revolution, or even of progress towards some revolutionary ideal in their own country. Instead they concentrate on achieving rapid economic and technological progress, by whatever means.

The current Chinese constitution, adopted in 1982, states: 'The basic task of the nation in the years to come is to concentrate its effort on socialist modernisation.' As 'modernisation' turned out to require a free market, free enterprise and foreign investment, that is what China's leaders have gone for. By 1997, a negotiated agreement between Britain and Communist China enabled the latter to take over the British colony of Hong Kong – one of the largest centres of global capitalism – without noticeably affecting its business activities. China now has one of the fastest growing economies in the world, but also has 40 million unemployed and a rural population flooding into the cities to provide cheap labour.

Capitalism and corruption

The forces unleashed by economic reform in China have been a challenge for the communist system to handle. There has been rampant corruption, inequality of wealth between winners and losers in the free market, and social dislocation on an epic

A Chinese farmer observes the Three Gorges dam under construction on the Yangzi River at the end of the twentieth century. Rapid economic growth and construction such as this brought about a massive upheaval in Chinese society, with millions of peasants and workers being forced to leave their homes and migrate in search of work.

Chinese materialism

According to China expert Jonathan D. Spence, the ambitions of the Chinese people reflected the changes that had taken place in the country after the death of Mao Zedong in 1976. Under Mao, it was said, people had aspired to the Four Musts: a bicycle, a radio, a watch and a sewing machine. But by the 1990s they wanted the Eight Bigs and the Three Highs. The Eight Bigs were: a colour TV, a refrigerator, a stereo, a camera, a motorbike, a suite of furniture, a washing machine and an electric fan. And the Three Highs were what a man needed to get a wife: a high salary, higher education, and a height of over 170 centimetres.

scale. Roughly 150 million Chinese peasants, displaced from the land, roamed in search of work, gravitating to China's fast-growing cities or heading abroad. China became one of the world's major sources of migrant workers. Many observers believed that freeing up the economy would inevitably lead to the need for Western-style political freedoms. Yet the party monopoly of power has continued into the twenty-first century and individual freedom, although much greater than in the time of Mao Zedong, remains restricted.

Political chaos

Meanwhile, in the former Soviet Union and Eastern Europe, the collapse of communism led in many areas to political chaos or economic decline. In Yugoslavia, for example, armed conflict raged between different ethnic groups as a country that had been successfully held together by communist government for almost half a century fell apart in the 1990s.

In Russia and most other 'successor states' of the former Soviet Union there was only a very imperfect form of democracy. The abandonment of the communist welfare state and the rapid collapse

The ending of communist rule in Yugoslavia in the 1990s led to the break-up of the country and warfare between its different peoples. Here, a Kosovan man weeps amid the ruins of his home town, destroyed in the conflict that pitted a Kosovan independence movement against the Serbian government in 1999.

of state-run industries has brought severe hardship for many people. Unemployment is widespread. In most of the territory of the former Soviet Union, average life expectancy has fallen sharply as poverty takes its toll of the old and the weak. Meanwhile, former communist officials and gangsters have made massive fortunes out of the privatisation of the economy.

Communism – the lesser of two evils?

It is evident that many of the problems of the former communist countries were inherited from the time of communist rule, which left a legacy of rundown factories, polluted cities, poor-quality housing and old technology. Yet, under the circumstances, it was natural that many people soon felt nostalgia for the security and relative equality of the communist period, even in places such as Poland and East Germany where communist rule had been least popular. Descendants of the old communist parties have become active in democratic politics and have won substantial support almost everywhere in the former Soviet bloc.

In the wider world, many of the issues originally addressed by Marxism continue to be relevant. Former Soviet dissident Aleksandr Solzhenitsyn said in 1993: 'Although the earthly ideal of Socialism-Communism has collapsed, the problems it purported [promised] to solve remain: the brazen use of social advantage and the inordinate power of money... '

❝ Everything the communists told us about socialism was false. Everything they told us about capitalism was true. ❞

Following the end of the Cold War, the above saying began to circulate in former communist states. Socialism had proved unfair to almost everyone, restricting freedom and depressing economic growth. However, after the fall of communism, many people found capitalism to be as unjust and exploitative as Marxist propaganda always said it was.

Timeline

1848	Karl Marx, with his associate Friedrich Engels, publishes *The Communist Manifesto*, calling for a workers' revolution to overthrow capitalism
1903	Vladimir Ilyich Lenin creates the Bolshevik Party, a movement of Russian Marxist revolutionaries
1914–18	The First World War devastates Europe
March 1917	The tsarist regime in Russia collapses
November 1917	Lenin leads a takeover of power in Russia by the Bolshevik Party (which soon changes its name to the Communist Party)
1919	The Third International or Comintern is founded in Russia to promote world revolution
1921	The Chinese Communist Party is founded
1923	The Soviet Union is officially founded, ruled by the Soviet Communist Party
1924	Lenin dies
1927	Chinese Nationalists attack the Chinese communists, starting a long and complex struggle for control of China
1929	Joseph Stalin achieves unchallenged power in the Soviet Union; he decides on a policy of rapid industrialisation and the forcing of peasants into collective farms
1932	Famine in the Ukraine, largely caused by Stalin's policies, kills millions
1934	Chinese communists led by Mao Zedong make the Long March to escape from their Nationalist enemies
December 1934	Stalin's reign of terror intensifies after the assassination of leading communist, Sergei Kirov
1937–38	Stalin has the majority of his country's senior army officers and leading communist politicians arrested and either executed or sent to prison camps
1939	The Soviet Union signs an agreement with Nazi Germany which includes a deal to divide up Poland between them
1941	Nazi Germany and its allies invade the Soviet Union; the Soviet Union becomes an ally of Britain and, slightly later, the United States
May 1945	The Second World War in Europe ends with the defeat of Nazi Germany; the forces of the Soviet Union control Europe as far west as the middle of Germany
1945–48	The Soviet Union establishes communist governments in areas under its control, including Poland, Czechoslovakia, East Germany and Hungary in Eastern Europe and North Korea in East Asia
1947	US President Harry S Truman commits the United States to halting the spread of communism – the Truman Doctrine
1949	Communist forces led by Mao Zedong win the civil war in China and take power in Beijing
1950–53	The Korean War pits troops from communist North Korea and China against the USA and its allies, who intervene in support of South Korea; the war ends with Korea still split between a communist North and non-communist South

1953	Stalin dies
1954	Vietnamese communists take power in North Vietnam after defeating the French colonialists occupying their country
1956	A major uprising against communist rule in Hungary is suppressed by Soviet tanks
1958–59	In China, the radical Great Leap Forward, intended by Mao to revolutionise China, ends up causing mass famine
1959	Guerrilla leader Fidel Castro takes power in Cuba and soon establishes a communist regime
1961	The Soviet Union and East German communists build the Berlin Wall, dividing communist East Berlin from capitalist West Berlin
1966	The great upheaval of the Cultural Revolution convulses Chinese society
1968	An attempt to establish a liberal form of communism in Czechoslovakia ends when the Soviet Union and its allies invade the country, restoring hardline communists to power
1975	After the victory of the communists in the Vietnam War, North and South Vietnam are united under communist rule; communists also come to power in neighbouring Laos and Cambodia
1975	In southern Africa, Angola and Mozambique become independent of Portuguese colonial rule; their Marxist governments are opposed by anti-Marxist movements backed by the United States and South Africa
1976	Mao Zedong dies, setting off a power struggle within the Chinese Communist Party
1978	Deng Xiaoping begins to lead China towards modernisation, accepting foreign investment and a limited degree of private enterprise
1979	The Soviet Union invades Afghanistan in an ultimately failed attempt to defend a Marxist Afghan government
1980–81	The Solidarity movement challenges communist rule in Poland
1985	Mikhail Gorbachev becomes the political leader of the Soviet Union
1987	Gorbachev embarks on a reform of the Soviet Union's economic and political system, with the slogans 'glasnost' and 'perestroika'
June 1989	Student protests in Tiananmen Square, Beijing, are suppressed by the Chinese armed forces with heavy bloodshed
September–December 1989	Communist regimes throughout Eastern Europe collapse in the face of popular protests; the Berlin Wall falls
August 1991	The Communist Party is banned in Russia after a failed *coup* attempt by hardline communist leaders.
December 1991	The Soviet Union ceases to exist, breaking up into its separate republics
1997	Chinese leader Deng Xiaoping dies, but the Chinese Communist Party agrees to continue free-market economic policies
2001	The United States declares North Korea a 'rogue state'

Glossary

Bolshevik in revolutionary Russia, a member of the group that formed a majority of the Social Democrat Party which seized power under Lenin

bureaucracy staff of government departments or large organisations such as the Communist Party

collective owned by, or participating in, a large group of people – as opposed to individual ownership or a private/family life

collective farm a large farm supposedly owned and run by the people who work on it, but in practice owned and run by the state

communal 'communal ownership' means property is owned by a group or a community instead of by individuals

commune a social unit in which people share property, responsibility for work and the fruits of their labour on an equal basis

conservative in politics, tending to keep things as they are

coup illegal seizure of power in a state

democracy a political system in which the government is elected by the people

dictatorship usually refers to the rule of an individual who exercises absolute power; in Marxist terminology, the 'dictatorship of the proletariat' refers to rule by the working class over the rest of society

economic system the way goods are produced and distributed in a particular society

élite a select group of people who have more power, wealth etc. than the rest of society

Great Depression term for a period from the late 1920s through the 1930s when there was mass unemployment in most countries and world trade collapsed

guerrilla a soldier who is not part of a regular army and takes part in ambushes, hit-and-run attacks and sabotage

hereditary inherited through a family – for example, when on a ruler's death power passes to his/her son or daughter

idealist a person who is inspired by lofty values or aspirations

industrialisation the development of large-scale factories using machinery

judiciary the system of law courts in a country and the judges that sit in them

liberals political groups putting a high value on individual rights and personal freedom

mobilise to enthuse and organise a mass of people for some form of action

monopoly exclusive possession of something – either property or power

nationalism loyalty to your own country or people; the desire for your nation to have its own independent government

paranoia an irrational fear caused by the feeling that people are plotting against you

propaganda information, often distorted, intended to promote a cause or persuade people to support a government or other organisation

Provisional Government the government that held power in Russia from March to November 1917; it was called 'provisional' because it was holding power until a democratically elected Constituent Assembly could decide on the country's future form of government

radical in politics, favouring extreme measures or fundamental change

reactionaries people opposed to revolution or to what is considered to be progress

revolution a thorough, usually violent, transformation of existing society

sabotage the deliberate destruction of equipment or machinery; saboteurs are people who carry out acts of sabotage

sanctions measures taken to try to force a country to change its policies, typically involving cutting off trade or investment

show trials fixed court trials not designed to find out whether the accused is innocent or guilty, but to demonstrate to the public the guilt of the accused and the power of the state

single-party state a state in which only one political party is allowed to operate, instead of many parties as in Western democracies (e.g. Republicans, Democrats, Greens etc. in the USA), giving voters no choice between different policies to vote for

social democrat someone who believes in socialism, democracy and individual freedom

Soviet bloc the Soviet Union and the group of countries allied to and dominated by it from the late 1940s to the late 1980s, including Poland, Czechoslovakia, Hungary and East Germany

Soviet Union officially known as the Union of Soviet Socialist Republics (USSR), the Soviet Union was a federation of fifteen republics, including the Russian Soviet Federated Socialist Republic, and the Ukrainian, Byelorussian, Georgian, Estonian, Latvian, Lithuanian, Uzbek and Kazakh Soviet Socialist Republics

trade union an organisation formed by a group of workers to stand up against their employers

Further Information

Books

Karl Marx, *The Communist Manifesto* (1848)
This is a surprisingly readable book that presents most of the basic ideas of communism with unsurpassed clarity. It is available in a range of paperback editions. Several Internet sites (for example, www.marxists.org) offer the complete text to download.

'Rius', *Marx for Beginners* and *Mao for Beginners* (Pantheon Books, 2003)
A lot of information provided in comic-book form.

Richard Appignanesi and Oscar Zarate, *Introducing Lenin and the Russian Revolution* (Icon Books, 2000)

George Orwell, *Animal Farm* (first published in 1946, reprinted in 1998 by Penguin Books)
A famous satire of communism in the form of a fairytale.

Jung Chang, *Wild Swans* (Flamingo, 1993)
A dramatic account of the experience of living in China in the twentieth century.

Paul Dowswell, *The Russian Revolution* (Hodder Children's Books, 2003)
A title in the *Days That Shook the World* series, chronicling events leading up to 25 October 1917, the day when the Bolsheviks seized power in Russia.

Websites

Surfing the Internet for entries on topics such as 'communism', 'Soviet Union' or 'Communist China' will throw up a wealth of interesting material. Young readers should always be aware, however, that much material on the Internet is presented from a heavily partisan viewpoint – that is, by people or organisations who are either strongly pro- or anti-communist.

http://www.gmu.edu – The Museum of Communism at the George Mason University site is dedicated to detailing the crimes of communism. It has much useful information, although some of its judgements should be approached with caution.

http://www.marxists.org – This site celebrates the Marxist tradition. It contains a wealth of original texts and documentary material.

http://www.spartacus.schoolnet.co.uk/Russia.htm – This site provides an excellent overview of the Russian Revolution and the history of the Soviet Union.

http://english.peopledaily.com.cn/constitution/constitution.html – This site provides the complete text of the Chinese Constitution. The first parts of the constitution are an interesting statement of the position of the current Chinese regime.

http://www.amnesty.org – The Amnesty International website provides up-to-date information on human rights abuses in communist-ruled countries.

Index